Present to: _____

From: _____

Date: _____

The Dad Who Fathered Me

Blessed are the poor in spirit,
for theirs is the kingdom of heaven.
Blessed are those who mourn,
for they will be comforted.
Blessed are the meek,
for they will inherit the earth.
Blessed are those who hunger
and thirst for righteousness,
for they will be filled.
Blessed are the merciful,
for they will be shown mercy.
Blessed are the pure in heart,
for they will see God.
Blessed are the peacemakers,
for they will be called children of God.

Mathew 5: 3-9

Printed in the United States of America.

ISBN-13: 978-0-9910361-1-0
ISBN-10: 0-9910361-1-0

The Dad
Who Fathered Me

Cherished Memories

Dr. Verna R. Benjamin-Lambert

Health Intelligence Books
Georgia

The pair of shoes that
I wear, were given to me
by a dad who paved the path
that guided my
life-long journey.

Dr. Verna R. Benjamin-Lambert

Table of Contents

Blessed are those who

are persecuted because of

righteousness,

for theirs is the kingdom

of heaven.

Mathew 5:10

Preface

With no blue print to assist you with the upbringing of a strong progeny of nine children, it's indeed credible that you and Mom have managed to do a hugely commendable job as parents. My first impulse was to write a book about all nine of us. Then, I quickly realized that with the diversity of experiences that each of us have had, our lives cannot be captured within the covers of one, single book. That narrowed my choice to one subject –

a book about – The Dad Who Fathered Me; the point from where our stories emerge.

I hope Dad, you enjoy reading this book as much as I enjoyed putting it together for you.

I also hope that my other readers will take delight in the contents of this book, and can find parallels in it running with their lives. Additionally, it is my wish that your life becomes as much of an inspiration for them, as it has been for your nine children, grand-children, great grandchildren and generations to come.

With love,

Verna

Who Is A Dad?

A dad is someone who
wants to catch you before you fall
but instead picks you up, brushes
you off, and lets you try again.

A dad is someone who
wants to keep you from making mistakes but
instead lets you find your own way, even
though his heart breaks in silence when you
get hurt.

A dad is someone who
holds you when you cry,
scolds you when you break the rules,
shines with pride when you succeed,
and has faith in you even when you fail...

Susan Ceylise

He has given food and provision

to those who reverently and

worshipfully fear Him;

He will remember His covenant

forever and imprint it

[on His mind].

Psalm 111: 5

The Happy Father

I can still hear the crackle of your laughter when I awake from slumber every morning. Your happiness is certainly contagious. Your laughter, as I remember, echoed through our home in the quaint village of Brandon Hill, Jamaica West Indies. To us, it sounded like the gurgle of a well-fed child; the sound of a free-flowing brook.

Yes, that contagious laughter brought music to our ears and reassured us that you

Verna and Dad

were around. Your vibes were so positive; you carried a spiritual aura around you like a protective shield that we could take shelter under. Nothing kept you down for a very long time. To be sure, you must have had your trials and disappointments, but we were always spared from seeing you wallow in self-pity or self-doubt.

I so vividly recall an incident when I was only about nine years old. As usual, you would take your daily morning tour of your sugarcane plantation. On this particular morning it had rained over-night causing the soil to be soft and muddy. The boots you wore were covered with red mud when you returned home. As I ran to greet you at the door you handed me the boots to clean. The job seemed monumental to me because I thought the boots were just too muddy to get clean. I soon came up with a brilliant idea! My inner voice spoke and said; "just get a pail of water and wash them, they will be clean in no time." I ran, fetched the water and off I went to complete the task of cleaning my Dad's boots. When the boots got clean, I had yet another awesome idea! The little voice spoke once more and said; "get the oven real hot and put them inside to dry." I thought, how cool! I did just that. As I ran off to get ready for school, I forgot the boots. It was about forty five minutes later that I ran back to the oven to get them. As I opened the door of the oven, I was greeted with the fresh aroma of leather. The boots were baked crisp with the fronts raised about an inch in the air. I was terrified! I always knew that my Dad was a forgiving man but looking at his field boots I had no idea what type of punishment I would face.

I showed the boots to Leah, the lady who aided in taking care of us, she informed me that my Dad would be very upset at me. I took the boots to where my Dad was sitting on the verandah. As I handed them to him, he took a look at the boots and started laughing so hard that he couldn't contain himself in the chair. He soon got up, walked the length of the verandah as he clapped his hands. It took me some time to adjust my emotion from being totally scared to being very happy. As of that day, because of my Dad's reaction to his burned boots, I developed an attachment to him that remains unbroken.

You had such a sunny optimism that Dad, I would like to imagine I inherited that particular strand of DNA from you. It insulates me from real and imaginary hurts and preserves my sanity. It has pulled me out of the blues whenever my chips were down. It has made me resilient and has given me the courage to dig my heals in against all odds. It has saved me from the unreasonableness of hate, anger and regret. It has freed my heart of contempt and malice. It has protected me from deadly illnesses. It has released my sagging spirit from the big and small troubles of life and prevented me from getting sucked into the downward spiral of crippling hopelessness. Yes, Dad it is your laughter that has helped me connect with my higher, and wiser self.

Thank you Dad for giving me this physical demonstration of happiness. Not a day passes by when I don't feel grateful for having received this gift from you. I totally agree with Anne Bryan Smollin when she wrote: "There's nothing like a good laugh. It tickles our very souls. Laughter is an activity of the heart. We scrunch our souls with negativity and a lack of enthusiasm, but laughter smooths them out. Laughter makes a noise so others can hear our feelings."

Blessed are you when people

insult you, persecute you and

falsely say all kinds of evil

against you because of me.

Rejoice and be glad, because

great is your reward in heaven,

for in the same way they

persecuted the prophets

who were before you.

Mathew 5:11-12

The Provider

Dad, I am quite convinced that as a young man you had no idea that you would one day be called upon to take care of such a big family. Amazingly, you have successfully managed to do so, even with your inelastic resources. I've heard you declare so many times; "I love all my children." I believe every word of that statement despite the challenges it posed with parenting such a diverse array of personalities.

Over these years, you have provided for us in so many wonderful ways. Ways that I do not wish to itemize here in this book because they are too numerous to recall. And the strange thing is, even with nine children you had enough to take care of us and so many others. I remember you telling me the story of your father, Euriah, who lost his vision shortly after he married his second wife Mary.

Grandfather Euriah was a kind and loving man with a warm heart. He kept a small kitchen garden in the backyard of his modest house and grew his own crop in order to be able to put food on the table and keep his house fires burning. I also remember him cutting the best dark red stripe sugar cane that I ever had. By the time I was eight years old he had lost his vision. By now, his wife Mary, was with him for just a few years before he completely lost his sight.

Your Dad Euriah was a proud man who believed that he had failed because he was now no longer able to provide for his wife, Mary. He met with you and expressed his incessant worry about what would happen to him and Mary. Dad, even though you had nine of us to provide for, you knew that you could not allow your father to live in penury. You promised grandfather that henceforth you would ensure that both him and Mary would be provided for. With the assistance of your brother, Zedikiah you kept your promise to your Dad and took care of him and Mary for as long as they lived.

Your keen sense of responsibility allowed me to understand the importance of not limiting my resources to just taking care of my immediate family but that I should also be open and willing to lend a helping hand to others in need. For that inspiration, I thank you Dad.

Picture of our family in the very early years

But remember the LORD your God, for it is he who gives you the ability to produce wealth, and so confirms his covenant, which he swore to your ancestors, as it is today. All of our skills and special talents that we use in our businesses are all given to us by God. He gives us the ability to make money and cut deals.

Deuteronomy 8:18 NIV

The Businessman

ad, for a man who did not receive any formal schooling beyond the 4th grade, you have done a remarkable job as a businessman. You remind me of a kindergarten student that told his mother he did not need to go back to school after he completed that particular grade. The child's reasoning was that, he learnt everything he needed to know in kindergarten. I bet you must have felt the same way when you left 4th grade. Amazingly,

you have managed to convince me as well that further schooling would have been counterproductive in your case. It would not have made you a better businessman.

Dad, in my opinion, what makes you an astute businessman is your ability to negotiate. I've watched you negotiate the price of goods for the haberdashery, your vehicles and many other items. No merchant of any caliber could talk you into doing anything that you did not feel comfortable doing. You bought and sold goods as you deemed fit. You sold what people needed, not what you wanted to sell, and there is a vast difference between those two practices. The amazing thing about your approach to doing business was that you were never greedy. Your products were never overpriced. You knew the fair price of every product and you stayed within the limits of what a customer could afford.

I recall suppliers flocking to you to sell cocoa, pimento and ginger. You had men in the field cutting and reaping acres of sugar cane that you owned. Not only did you run all these operations simultaneously and smoothly, you also effectively operated the haberdashery with Mom by your side. You had a keen sense of knowing when to deliver goods to the merchants in Kingston. I also recall you asking Mom her opinion regarding the timing of selling the stockpile of ginger that you had dried and stored in the building that stood next to the store. There was even a time when a whole room of the house was taken over by ginger.

Then there was a time when the same individuals who sold you products stole from you but that did not throw your business off gear. One incident that sticks out in my memory scape is that fateful night when the men who worked for you bagged the ginger and loaded the packed bags on the truck that was to leave in the wee hours the of the morning for Kingston. Prior to loading, I saw the men use a blade of grass to test the tires to ensure that there was enough air in them. They made a huge, hissing sound that I found quite exciting.

I was so fascinated by this trick so I waited until the men loaded all the trucks and left for the evening. Then, I quietly sneaked into the yard where the dispatch trucks stood. While there were no onlookers, I mimicked what the men had done to test the tires. While bursting with glee and excitement, I listened to the sound until the air was all gone from every tire.

The next morning when the men returned to leave with the delivery consignment, they found all the tires flat. They identified me as the culprit and Dad, you were so upset with me, you fell on me like a ton of bricks. I got a spanking, the memory of which I can't forget to this day. Lesson learned! I knew I had to stay away from those trucks.

That lesson also allowed me to be a thinker. My actions as of that day have been tempered by thought. Never again did you have to scold me in that way.

That said, the manner in which you handled your business affairs has provided me with a template for conducting my interaction with business associates today. I must say, I enjoyed the time I spent with you in the haberdashery, purchasing local farmers' produce and offering them a fair price for it. I enjoyed riding in the car with you as you visited neighboring districts to visit business associates. And of course, I loved to count your earnings at the end of each working day. Even though you succeeded at being your own boss throughout the years, with very little formal schooling you never once discouraged any of your children from attaining the highest level of education they wanted to. I guess you not only understood the value of money but you also knew the importance of having a good education. You gave us choices for which we will always remain grateful to you.

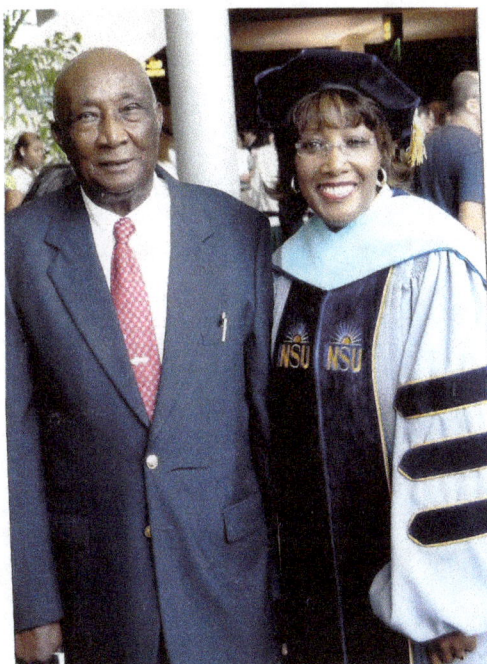

Verna's Graduation from Nova Southeastern University

For I have chosen him, that he may command his children and his household after him to keep the way of the LORD by doing righteousness and justice, so that the LORD may bring to Abraham what he has promised him."

Genesis 18:19

The Teacher

I observed your kindness and the many hours you spent reading scriptures to your children during the wee hours of the morning. It made us appreciate that our Dad's life was totally guided by a higher

> *Train up a child in the way he should go; even when he is old he will not depart from it.*
>
> Proverbs 22:6

power. Your faith in the Lord was grounded in your unfailing love of Jesus Christ.

Through your teachings, I've found the true meaning of life. It has allowed me to understand that a fulfilled life lies in discovering and embracing what brings joy to the heart; peace of mind; humility of spirit; gratitude; love for others; acknowledgment and thanks to God for his goodness and all-sustaining love.

Even though we spent hours with you as you taught us the word of God, I must articulate that most of your unforgettable instructions came from the way you conducted yourself in front of your children. You set the example that we devotedly followed. I learned to read and study the word of God from watching you lovingly delve into the scriptures. I thought, since you loved reading the Bible so much it had to be good for me as well. You taught me to pray in humility as I watched you and heard the tremble in your voice as you broke in reverence while praying on your knees. It was only during those highly emotive times that I saw tears rolling down your cheeks.

I often wondered why you cried and in my childlike naivety I imagined that praying made you sad. For a brief time, I stopped praying because I did not want to be a part of anything that made you sad. Then one day when you arose from your knees I asked: "Dad why do you cry when you pray?" You calmly placed your hand on my shoulders, looked deep into my eyes and replied. "I am not really crying, the tears flow because my heart is full of love for God and I am thankful for his goodness."

I understood then and never questioned your love for God. As of that day and from that moment, praying became a part of my daily life.

Through your work ethic you taught me independence. You waited for no one to employ you but gave employment to others. By your own example, you showed me the importance of respecting everyone, regardless of their color, economic status or religious beliefs. Yes, I learned how to disagree without engaging in hateful exchanges. It is from you that I learned that staying quiet can be a mark of strength and not weakness.

You taught me to embrace the poor and share with everyone, especially the needy. I learnt that a poor mind is more destructive than the lack of financial resources. You made me believe that through education anyone can be whatever they want to be. I believed it then, and am even more convinced of that dictum now.

You taught me to give, and to express grace and gratitude in receiving. I saw you as a man who enjoyed giving more than how you enjoyed receiving. You gave aplenty of yourself—spiritually, emotionally, financially and served everyone with honor and dignity.

I am so fortunate to have a role model like you in my life.

Verna and Dad

Do nothing from selfish ambition or conceit, but in humility count others more significant than yourselves. Let each of you look not only to his own interests, but also to the interests of others. Have this mind among yourselves, which is yours in Christ Jesus, who, though he was in the form of God, did not count equality with God a thing to be grasped, but emptied himself, by taking the form of a servant being born in the likeness of men. And being found in human form, he humbled himself by becoming obedient to the point of death, even death on a cross.

Philippians 2:3-8

I have showed you all things,

how that so laboring ye ought

to support the weak, and to

remember the words of the

Lord Jesus, how he said,

It is more blessed to give than

to receive.

Acts 20:35

The
Servant-Leader

*D*ad, your life reflects that of a servant-leader. A servant leader, in my understanding is one who possesses the ability to listen; has empathy for others; facilitates healing relationships; is always aware of what is happening with, or to others; has the power of persuasion; has the ability to conceptualize and appropriately apply solutions to issues of concern to others; possesses foresight; understands stewardship; shows commitment to human development; and dreams of building a strong, ethically-guided community. All these attributes you had and practiced in your life.

When I look back, I observe that your life has been one of utter selflessness. As you sat on the verandah of our home, I recall the poor, the teachers, ministers, other businessmen, politicians and others flocking to our home to converse with you or seek guidance. Your wisdom transcended that of any scholar. Although you are ninety years old now, your mind is still sharp and the knowledge that flows from your spiritually enriched mind creates inspiration for others. I often wonder why we had to share you with so many people. However, I kept those thoughts to myself because you seemed to relish every moment of the company of those people, who sought you out.

I so vividly recall a woman who once came to our house weeping with bruises and swellings on her face and arms. I had seen her before and knew who she was. It was evident that she had been abused and beaten by some evil and uncaring person. As I stood looking on in a state of despair, I heard her telling you that her husband had beaten her after arriving home in a drunken state. Dad, you looked at her and with a deep sigh of pity and mumbled: "How could any- one in his right mind do something like this?" Thereafter, the woman wept inconsolably while you shook your head and offered her words of comfort. You told her that God will deliver her and she should put her trust in him.

Mom and Dad

Dad, you were never the one to advise any- one to fight fire with fire. You summoned Mom who was forever busy making sure her children were being cared for appropriately. She responded and entered the living room to hear what you had to say. As Mom approached the woman, it was evident that you did not need to say anything. The battered woman stood there weeping hopelessly.

Mom hugged her and whispered in her ear; "Don't worry you are going to be Ok". She then ushered her to the bathroom to clean her wounds and put layers of ointment on them. She offered her a place to rest until she decided what she wanted to do next. The woman stayed with us for a few hours and left after eating a meal that Francis, the cook, had prepared for her at Mom's request. There were many more times that I saw you show such deep feelings of concern for family and friends.

Dad, you have always been an excellent listener. You were never too busy to stop whatever you were doing to ensure that you acknowledged whatever or whoever needed your urgent attention. You always communicated with kindness and compassion. Your probing questions were asked to ensure that the listener's response would be right. You were honest

yet sensitive. Dad you stayed in touch with
your soul and spoke truth from its center. Your
spiritual existence served as a compass for the
way you related and interacted with everyone
around you.

Since there was no definite means of trans-
portation in the village, you were often called
upon to transport the sick to the doctor or
hospital. Night after night, villagers in trouble
would knock on your door for help. As a child,
I used to get quite upset to see my Dad leave
my Mom in bed to chaperon these people to
the hospital and elsewhere. I often wondered
why Mom did not stop you. Somehow my
childish selfishness did not allow me to understand that you found your life purpose to
serve others in need. Thank God my Mom understood your true purpose. There were times
when you had to forego a night of rest because
when you returned it would be time to go on
to the place of business.

The incident that left a huge impact on me
was when you responded to a pregnant woman's call for help. It was about 3:00 am when
her husband came to seek your assistance.
You seemed frightened and nervous. Sensing

the urgency of the situation, you jumped out of bed, got dressed and told Mom that you would be back soon.

The hospital was about an hour's drive away. The unpaved roads did not allow you to speed above twenty-five to thirty-five miles per hour. About half way through the winding, hilly and rock covered road, Mrs. Cole's baby started to descend through the birth canal. I do not know the rest of the story about this child but I recall you returning to the house parking the car and summoning Mom to your side.

A few moments later, we all heard the cry of the newborn. I was scared and did not know what was happening. I am not sure how Mrs. Cole got in one of our bedrooms but you and Mom allowed her and the baby to stay at the house for seven days until they thought it was safe for the baby and mother to go home. The empathy you showed for others made you a favorite among the people in the village and beyond.

As your farm flourished, you were able to hire the young men in the village to take care of the various cows, pigs and the cane field. The men would be happy when it was time to reap the sugar cane because their paychecks would be guaranteed for at least the next three to four months of the year. More hands got hired during the cane season than any other.

I would see you happily give men advances either by prepaying them or allowing them to get supplies from the store on credit until they got paid. If they came asking for more, you went giving. You surely have a heart of pure gold. There were times when you never got back what you had extended because for various reasons some of the workers would disappear before they were able to repay their loan or satisfy the credit that you had extended.

Dad, at times you would rationalize the disappearance of workers by saying "I wonder what is wrong?" "I hope he will be back soon." A few would return but some did not. However, you never held a grudge against anyone. When I once asked you about the long list of uncollected balances, you told me it was "Ok" and I should not worry about it. You took pains to explain to me that some people do not have the mind to do what is right.

Your ability to support various charity organizations was unmatched by anyone else in the village. You would serve as a juror on many occasions. You strongly believed in rehabilitating offenders of the law. Your empathic mind did not allow you to be very harsh as you participated in making decisions within the guidelines of the law. The many years you serve as Justice of the Peace allows you to serve in a capacity that at times leaves you physically drained and tired. However, I never saw you turn anyone away because you didn't have the will or the energy to serve your fellowmen in need.

Mom and Dad

In accordance with your great love, forgive the sin of these people, just as you have pardoned them from the time they left Egypt until now." The LORD replied, "I have forgiven them, as you asked.

Numbers 14: 19-21

"This, then, is how you should pray:

"'Our Father in heaven, hallowed be your name, your kingdom come, your will be done on earth as it is in heaven. Give us today our daily bread. Forgive us our debts, as we also have forgiven our debtors. And lead us not into temptation, but deliver us from the evil one. ' For if you forgive men when they sin against you, your heavenly Father will also forgive you. But if you do not forgive men their sins, your Father will not forgive your sins.

Mathew 6:9-15

The Forgiver

Throughout the years Dad, your ability to forgive others caused me to believe that you have attained sainthood. I am not sure when or how your spiritual enlightenment occurred. However, the one thing that I am sure about is that you possess the true characteristic of a man who understands how to live life in complete balance. You have fed your body well. You keep your soul refreshed and nourished. You are spiritually enlightened. It is evident that because you have always guided your life by the teachings of Jesus Christ, your ability to forgive is exemplary.

I vividly recall an incident that occurred at a very early age when someone from the village broke into the family haberdashery to steal leather. Another villager saw the break-in and rushed to our home to alert you. I saw the fear in your eyes as you thanked the informant and then rushed out to catch the burglary in progress.

Luckily, you got to the shop in time to see the burglar about to exit. You approached the thief and directed him to leave the leather. The burglar turned and attempted to use a long bladed sharp knife to stab you. This was quite a scary confrontational moment I am sure. But Dad you quickly grabbed his wrist and held him by the neck, at which time the burglar dropped the weapon. Later, the police whisked him away and locked him in the jail.

This must have been a very frightening encounter for you. When you shared the experience with Mom upon returning home, she was quite alarmed and inquired if you were OK. You convinced her that you were fine.

Mom shared the news with Leah.

I was only about six years old then, so neither Mom nor you were aware that I was eavesdropping and could understand the close shave with death that you en-countered. It made me sad. Because of my deep love for you, Dad, I could not bear the thought of you ever being hurt. As I gazed at you with tears welled up in my eyes, I could see you were deep in thought. I do not think you were aware then that I was intensely watching you because once again I did not make my presence known.

I soon heard you call, "Ms. Benji."

This was the name you use to address Mom.

She immediately responded: "Yes Ben;"

"I will be back soon," you shouted so that she could hear you in the adjoining room.

She quickly rushed to where you were standing and implored, "Why don't you rest a few hours before you leave?"

But Dad, you assured her that you were fine and that you would be back soon.

When you returned, you informed Mom that you went to visit the police station to request for the burglar to be released. You had decided not to press charges against the accused because you had forgiven him for what he had done. I was amazed when I heard you recount this incident to Mom. Mom stepped close to you, hugged you and silently walked away. It was apparent that my mother was not surprised at what her Ben had done, because she knew the man she married better than anyone else and knew this gesture was an integral feature of your character.

Many years later when I got married and was treated terribly by a man who did not deserve me as his partner; Dad you counseled me to forgive him because in time, I would understand that God will intercede on my behalf. I listened and believed what you told me. Today, I must report that I am so much better off for taking your advice.

Through these years, many despicable moments of heart break and disappointments have come to you Dad, and your family for whom you care so deeply, but you never allowed yourself to nurse a grudge against anyone. Your spirit remained refreshed and renewed; causing you to rise above the bitterness and hate that would have crushed a lesser man's soul.

I so vividly recall the unthinkable that happened soon after your semi-retirement. It was a time when the political climate in Jamaica prompted thugs and criminals to imagine that honest work was no longer a requirement. It was a time when your faith in God was severely tested. I could hear your heart chanting David's song of praise:

[2] Samuel 22:2-7; "The LORD is my rock, my fortress and my deliverer;

[3] my God is my rock, in whom I take refuge, my shield[a] and the horn[b] of my salvation.
He is my stronghold, my refuge and my savior—
from violent people you save me.

[4] "I called to the LORD, who is worthy of praise,
and have been saved from my enemies.

[5] The waves of death swirled about me;
   the torrents of destruction overwhelmed
   me.
[6] The cords of the grave coiled around me;
   the snares of death confronted me.
[7] "In my distress I called to the LORD;
   I called out to my God.
   From his temple he heard my voice;
   my cry came to his ears.

And with that, you moved on with the understanding that God is in control and nothing will separate you from his love. I could also hear your heart song: "In moments like these I raise up my voice and sing out a love song to Jesus, singing I love you Lord."

You make known to me the path of life; you will fill me with joy in your presence, with eternal pleasures at your right hand.

Psalm 16:11

Memories Captured

Grandma, Grandpa,
and all the girls

Dad, Lauren,
Harry, and Verna

Grandpa, Nadia
& Lauren

Grandpa and the girls

Dad, Lauren, and Verna

Benjamin Galloway,
Nadia & Kenya's Son

Mom, Nadia, Nicole,
Melissa, & Lauren
at Nadia's Wedding
November 27, 2004

Harry, Isaac, & Kenya

Lauren and Grandpa in her early years

Dad, Mom, & Lauaren

Lauren and Grandpa

Harry and Verna

Harry, Kenya, Isaac, Christian,
Harrison, Benjamin, & Ian

Melissa (1st Grandchild)

Nicole, Isaac, Grandma, Grandpa,
Mom, & Dad

Nadia and Kenya's Wedding
November 27, 2004

Verna, Harry, and
the Grandchildren

Nicole & Nadia Operators
of The Benjamin
Preschool of Academics
& Performing Arts

I appeal to you therefore,

brothers, by the mercies of God,

to present your bodies as a living

sacrifice, holy and acceptable

to God, which is your spiritual

worship. Do not be conformed to

this world, but be transformed by

the renewal of your mind, that

by testing you may discern what

is the will of God, what is good

and acceptable and perfect.

Romans 12:1-2

Worshiper

*D*ad, you have consistently prayed for blessings upon your children. I have often watched you weep as you knelt in homage to our maker. Your love and commitment to God was one that no one could question. You would often talk about King David as a living person of flesh and blood. You saw yourself in him because of the way he expressed his love for God and to God. Please understand Dad, that if David was considered a man after God's own heart, I must say that you too fall in the same bracket of worthy worshippers. Your brother David's moral standing fell short, at times but not yours.

Dad Praying At Harrisons Christening in Jamaica (88 years old)

Dad, your many examples of faithfulness and dedication to your mate has guided my relationships. You have caused me to stand on the stage of life without making any excuses for the way I chose to live my life. Your high standards in all aspects of life have caused me to take second place to no one. My focus has been steadfast; my goals never seemed unreachable; I wanted to be like no one else but myself; and the only people I wanted to please in life were you and my Mom. I understand now that I am fortunate to have the best role models and for that I will forever be grateful to God.

Today, as you have been blessed with long life, I cannot express how happy I am to be here with you on this your ninetieth birthday. Look at you! You still stand tall. You still eat well! You still do your own banking and you still laugh like no one else does!

We your children can rise up and call you blessed. Dad, keep laughing; keep praying and I don't need to tell you - keep being humble at the feet of Jesus.

There is no doubt that I could not have written a better script by which to guide my life. Thank you. Thank you. Thank you. May God continue to be good to you.

Love you Dad!

Keep me as the apple of your eye;

hide me in the shadow of your wings

Psalm 17:8

The Preacher

Dad, as a child I looked forward to hearing you preach. The lucid manner in which you delivered inspirational messages, enabled me to make sense of the world around me and instilled a deep sense of love and longing for God almighty. I felt deep pride and happiness as I hung on to every syllable that you spoke. I wondered how you knew the things you said. As I grew older, I watched you reading your Bible and praying as you got ready for your sermons, and something told me that you were sharing your thoughts with God during those quiet moments.

Your sermons were not filled with fear as those of other preachers but rather, they were sermons of hope, love and grace. You spoke convincingly about the coming of the Lord. You preached of Moses, Elijah, Joshua, Job, Paul and David. You preached of the prophets and kings. You preached straight out of the heart of God. Yes, you told the people to be watchful and implored them not to grow weary.

You spoke with a knowing and did not once sound apologetic for spreading the word of God. Your teachings helped me to know what kindness and mercy meant. I saw your heart and knew early on in my life that it was pure as gold.

Dad, the preacher

Scriptures From Dad's Sermons

Psalm 1

Blessed is the one who does not walk in step
with the wicked
or stand in the way that sinners take
or sit in the company of mockers,
but whose delight is in the law of the LORD,
and who meditates on his law day and night.
That person is like a tree planted by streams of
water,
which yields its fruit in season
and whose leaf does not wither—
whatever they do prospers.

Not so the wicked!
They are like chaff
that the wind blows away.
Therefore the wicked will not stand in the
judgment,
nor sinners in the assembly of the righteous.

For the LORD watches over the way of the
righteous,
but the way of the wicked leads to destruction.

Ecclesiastes 5

New International Version (NIV)

Fulfill Your Vow to God

Guard your steps when you go to the house of God. Go near to listen rather than to offer the sacrifice of fools, who do not know that they do wrong.

Do not be quick with your mouth,
do not be hasty in your heart
to utter anything before God.
God is in heaven
and you are on earth,
so let your words be few.
A dream comes when there are many cares,
and many words mark the speech of a fool.

When you make a vow to God, do not delay to fulfill it. He has no pleasure in fools; fulfill your vow. [5] It is better not to make a vow than to make one and not fulfill it. [6] Do not let your mouth lead you into sin. And do not protest to the temple messenger, "My vow was a mistake." Why should God be angry at what you say and destroy the work of your hands? [7] Much dreaming and many words are meaningless. Therefore fear God.

1 Corinthians 12

New International Version (NIV)

Concerning Spiritual Gifts

12 Now about the gifts of the Spirit, brothers and sisters, I do not want you to be uninformed. [2] You know that when you were pagans, somehow or other you were influenced and led astray to mute idols. [3] Therefore I want you to know that no one who is speaking by the Spirit of God says, "Jesus be cursed," and no one can say, "Jesus is Lord," except by the Holy Spirit.

There are different kinds of gifts, but the same Spirit distributes them. [5] There are different kinds of service, but the same Lord.

There are different kinds of working, but in all of them and in everyone it is the same God at work.

Now to each one the manifestation of the Spirit is given for the common good. To one there is given through the Spirit a message of wisdom, to another a message of knowledge by means of the same Spirit, to another faith by the same Spirit, to another gifts of healing by that one Spirit, to another miraculous powers, to another prophecy, to another distinguishing between spirits, to another speaking in different kinds of tongues, and to still another the interpretation of tongues. All these are the work of one and the same Spirit, and he distributes them to each one, just as he determines.

Matthew 5

New International Version (NIV)

Introduction to the Sermon on the Mount

Now when Jesus saw the crowds, he went up on a mountainside and sat down. His disciples came to him, and he began to teach them.

Romans 5

New International Version (NIV)

Peace and Hope

Therefore, since we have been justified through faith, we have peace with God through our Lord Jesus Christ, [2] through whom we have gained access by faith into this grace in which we now stand. And we boast in the hope of the glory of God. Not only so, but we also glory in our sufferings, because we know that suffering produces perseverance; perseverance, character; and character, hope. And hope does not put us to shame, because God's love has been poured out into our hearts through the Holy Spirit, who has been given to us.

You see, at just the right time, when we were still powerless, Christ died for the ungodly. Very rarely will anyone die for a righteous person, though for a good person someone might possibly dare to die. But God demonstrates his own love for us in this: While we were still sinners, Christ died for us.

Since we have now been justified by his blood, how much more shall we be saved from God's wrath through him! For if, while we were God's enemies, we were reconciled to him through the death of his Son, how much more, having been reconciled, shall we be saved through his life! Not only is this so, but we also boast in God through our Lord Jesus Christ, through whom we have now received reconciliation.

1 Timothy 6: 11-21

Final Charge to Timothy

But you, man of God, flee from all this, and pursue righteousness, godliness, faith, love, endurance and gentleness. Fight the good fight of the faith. Take hold of the eternal life to which you were called when you made your good confession in the presence of many witnesses. In the sight of God, who gives life to everything, and of Christ Jesus, who while testifying before Pontius Pilate made the good confession, I charge you to keep this command without spot or blame until the appearing of our Lord Jesus Christ, which God will bring about in his own time—God, the blessed and only Ruler, the King of kings and Lord of lords, who alone is immortal and who lives in unapproachable light, whom no one has seen or can see. To him be honor and might forever. Amen.

Command those who are rich in this present world not to be arrogant nor to put their hope in wealth, which is so uncertain, but to put their hope in God, who richly provides

us with everything for our enjoyment.
Command them to do good, to be rich in
good deeds, and to be generous and willing
to share. In this way they will lay up treasure
for themselves as a firm foundation for the
coming age, so that they may take hold of the
life that is truly life.

Timothy, guard what has been entrusted to
your care. Turn away from godless chatter
and the opposing ideas of what is falsely
called knowledge, which some have professed
and in so doing have departed from the faith.

Grace be with you all.

Ephesians 5

New International Version (NIV)

Follow God's example, therefore, as dearly
loved children and walk in the way of love,
just as Christ loved us and gave himself up
for us as a fragrant offering and sacrifice to
God.

But among you there must not be even a hint of sexual immorality, or of any kind of impurity, or of greed, because these are improper for God's holy people. Nor should there be obscenity, foolish talk or coarse joking, which are out of place, but rather thanksgiving. For of this you can be sure: No immoral, impure or greedy person—such a person is an idolater—has any inheritance in the kingdom of Christ and of God. Let no one deceive you with empty words, for because of such things God's wrath comes on those who are disobedient. Therefore do not be partners with them.

For you were once darkness, but now you are light in the Lord. Live as children of light (for the fruit of the light consists in all goodness, righteousness and truth) and find out what pleases the Lord. Have nothing to do with the fruitless deeds of darkness, but rather expose them. It is shameful even to mention what the disobedient do in secret. But everything exposed by the light becomes visible—and everything that is illuminated becomes a light. This is why it is said:

"Wake up, sleeper,
rise from the dead,
and Christ will shine on you."

Be very careful, then, how you live—not as unwise but as wise, making the most of every opportunity, because the days are evil. Therefore do not be foolish, but understand what the Lord's will is. Do not get drunk on wine, which leads to debauchery. Instead, be filled with the Spirit, speaking to one another with psalms, hymns, and songs from the Spirit. Sing and make music from your heart to the Lord, always giving thanks to God the Father for everything, in the name of our Lord Jesus Christ.

Instructions for Christian Households

Submit to one another out of reverence for Christ.

Wives, submit yourselves to your own husbands as you do to the Lord. For the husband is the head of the wife as Christ is the head of the church, his body, of which he is the Savior. Now as the church submits to Christ, so also wives should submit to their husbands in everything.

Husbands, love your wives, just as Christ loved the church and gave himself up for her to make her holy, cleansing her by the washing with water through the word, and to present her to himself as a radiant church, without stain or wrinkle or any other blemish, but holy and blameless. In this same way, husbands ought to love their wives as their own bodies. He who loves his wife loves himself. After all, no one ever hated their own body, but they feed and care for their body, just as Christ does the church— for we are members of his body. "For this reason a man will leave his father and mother and be united to his wife, and the two will become one flesh." This is a profound mystery—but I am talking about Christ and the church. However, each one of you also must love his wife as he loves himself, and the wife must respect her husband.

A Psalm For Giving Thanks

Make a joyful noise to the Lord, all the earth! Serve the Lord with gladness! Come into his presence with singing! Know that the Lord, he is God! It is he who made us, and we are his; we are his people, and the sheep of his pasture. Enter his gates with thanksgiving, and his courts with praise! Give thanks to him; bless his name! For the Lord is good; his steadfast love endures forever, and his faithfulness to all generations

Psalm 100:1-5 ESV

A Grateful
Heart

ad, you have been there for me throughout my life. You gave me complements that others did not hear. You encouraged me each time I crossed a big or small milestone. You listened to me speak and told me how proud you were of how I presented myself. You were there for my first graduation ceremony from St. Joseph's Teachers' College

67

in Jamaica, West Indies and of course, as promised you traveled from Jamaica to attend my graduation when I completed my doctoral degree at Nova Southeastern University in the United States.

I knew that you had no interest in traveling at the time but because you had promised me that whenever I completed my doctorial degree you would not miss that day; yes Dad, you kept your promise and I was so happy that you and Mom were there to witness me walk across the stage to receive my degree.

You were there to walk me down the aisle when I got married. You prayed and comforted me when the vow of faithfulness with my partner was broken. You traveled to the United Sates on various occasions and spent time with my family. You even predicted the career of one of my children when she was barely eight years old. Again you made the commitment that if she became a lawyer, as you predicted, you would be sure to attend her graduation. It so happened that when Nicole graduated from Yale University and went on to earn her JD degree at Georgetown University in the United States both you and Mom were there to see her graduate. That is the kind of father and grandfather you have been – true to your words!

You might recall a conversation we had after I graduated from St Joseph's and was assigned to do my teaching internship in Wakefield, Trelawney, Jamaica, and West Indies. I promised you then that the only way that I would be able to repay you for what you had done to assist me in my success, would be to do the same for my children. With that promise in mind, I made a very calculated and conscious decision to guide my four children

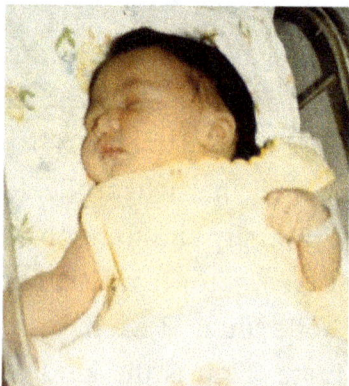

Najwa Sade'
August 21, 1986 –
January 11, 1987

throughout their lives. Dad today, I believe that I have been successful in the way I have parented all my four girls. Without you and Mom providing a compass for me to use to guide my parenting path, I would not have been able to create the balance that I have for my children.

Of course, there were challenging times especially in the death of one of my children, Najwa, who went to be with the Lord at the tender age of five months old, the first child between Harry, my second husband, and I. Of course you must have understood the valley that I found myself in and the unanswered questions that pierced my soul. I overcame this difficult time only because of the teachings that you imparted to me during my early years, and through the voice of the Lord that spoke to me explaining the reason for her departure from this life. Neither you, nor Mom had experienced such acute pain but when I thought and asked myself what would you have done in my situation, your calm comforting voice within me recalled a song I heard you and Mom sang ever so frequently;

I've found a friend in Jesus

I have found a friend in Jesus, He's everything to me,
He's the fairest of ten thousand to my soul
The Lily of the Valley, in Him alone I see
All I need to cleanse and make me fully whole.
In sorrow He's my comfort,
in trouble He's my stay;
He tells me every care on Him to roll.

Refrain

He's the Lily of the Valley, the Bright and Morning Star,
He's the fairest of ten thousand to my soul.

He all my grief has taken, and all my sorrows borne;
In temptation He's my strong and mighty tower;
I have all for Him forsaken, and all my idols torn
From my heart and now
He keeps me by His power.
Though all the world forsake me,
and Satan tempt me sore,
Through Jesus I shall safely reach the goal.

Refrain

He will never, never leave me, nor yet forsake me here,
While I live by faith and do His blessèd will;
A wall of fire about me, I've nothing now to fear,
From His manna He my hungry soul shall fill.
Then sweeping up to glory to see His blessèd face,
Where the rivers of delight shall ever roll.

Refrain

Charles W. Fry, 1881

Years later when my second daughter Nicole and her husband, Isaac, were faced with the sudden and untimely passing of their first born son, Isaac, Jr. at six months old, she shared with me that she gathered her strength from living through the similar experience as I did.

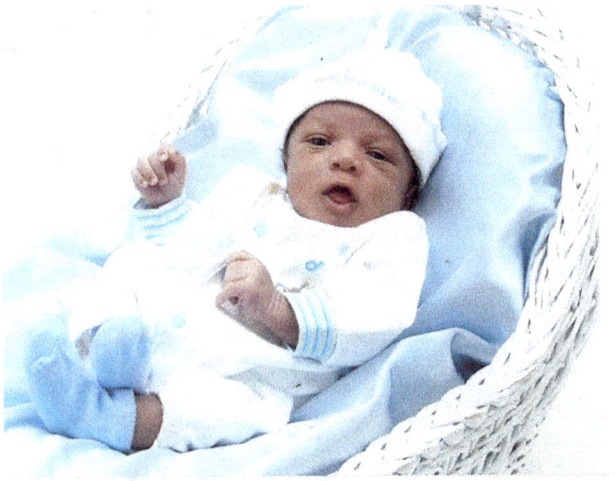

Isaac DeWayne Kelly, Jr.
July 27, 2007 to January 27, 2008

She articulated; "Mom if you could, I can." Her resilience was remarkable. I still stand in awe of her strength. She too "found grace in the eye of the storm." Thank you Dad for setting the tone that would supply me with the resource that our family needed in those

Melissa

Nicole

Naida

Lauren

dark hours. You are an exceptional father. Your grandchildren, Melissa, Nicole, Nadia and Lauren have grown up to be strong individuals who continue to contribute much to their peers, and society as whole. Nicole is the mother of three boys, Ian, Christian and Harrison. Nadia has one child who carries the family name, Benjamin. We pray that the pebbles of your teachings will continue to be passed down to your off springs for generations to come and that they will all, by God's grace, have a place in His kingdom. This I know is the desire of your and Mom's heart.

Benjamin

A Father's Treasure

"Don't you see

that children are God's best gift,

the fruit of the womb

his generous legacy?

Like a warrior's fistful of arrows

are the children of a vigorous youth.

Oh, how blessed are you parents,

with your quivers full of children!

Your enemies

don't stand a chance against you;

you'll sweep them right off

your doorstep."

Palm 127: 3-5, MSG

A Tribute to
My Father

The legacy that my father has built for us in these ninety years, cannot be measured in years. Nor can it be measured in words or verses.

It can only be treasured and that's what I have attempted to do with this book. When I opened The Benjamin Preschool of Academics and Performing Arts in Smyrna, Georgia, three

years ago and named it in his honor, I meant it to be a tribute to my Dad. The school is now being operated by two of his granddaughters, Nicole Kelly and Nadia Galloway with me serving in the capacity of Principal Amaritus.

Three of his great grandchildren, Ian, Christian and Harrison are students at the school.

As you can see, Dad, your legacy lives on. With all my love,

Verna

MY DADDA'S MANTLE

Oh Dad you hold the mantle in your hand with flames that penetrates the dark
It served to guide me through the night and lasted till morning light
You took me on a path where others might not have trod
You never wavered or grew tired; you knew you were the appointed one
Inspired by your maker you guided me to my destiny

REFRAIN

Where oh where did you learn how to laugh and when to cry
When oh when did you know that you were the chosen one
Why oh why you treated me so kind so that I could find joy and learn how to fly

How oh how I can't explain my thanks to you for being there

I have lived my life without excuse because I knew I was led by the truth
Your thoughtfulness and love served to heal my broken wounds
Your laughter echoes through my soul telling me I am never oh never alone
Yes you are, yes you are , yes you are the chosen one

Where oh where did you learn how to laugh and when to cry
When oh when did you know that you were the chosen one
Why oh why you treated me so kind so that I

could find joy and learn how to fly
How oh how I can't explain my thanks to you for
being there

VERSE

Now the grace of God in me flows like living
water from above
my soul is satisfied as I give thanks to God for
you loving me
Your strong shoulders on which I stand allows me
to soar through the skies
I see the mountains and the hills and shout
praises unto God, oh praises,
oh praises, oh praises onto God
Thank you, thank you, thank you Dad for the
flaming mantle
Thank you, thank you, thank you.

REFRAIN

Where oh where did you learn how to laugh and when to cry

When oh when did you know that you were the chosen one

Why oh why you treated me so kind so that I could find joy and learn how to fly

How oh how I can't explain my thanks to you for being there

Dr. Verna R. Benjamin-Lambert

October 10, 2013

About the Author

"No child on this earth is here by accident. Every child has a soul, and every soul has a purpose. If children's emotional, educational, spiritual, physical and financial needs are met they will be able to achieve at their highest potential."
Dr. Verna R. Benjamin-Lambert

*D*r. Verna R. Benjamin-Lambert has dedicated her life to serving children. Her tireless passion in helping the youth is fueled by her strong belief that given a chance, every child can experience success.

Dad and Dr. Verna

A graduate of St. Joseph's Teachers' College in her native country of Jamaica, West Indies, she migrated to the United States, where she worked in the private sector before returning to the classroom. Her studies at Kennesaw State University in Psychology and West Georgia University in Special Education Leadership gave her the tools to become an advocate for students with disabilities. Following her undergraduate studies, she went on to obtain her doctorate in

Education Leadership from the Nova Southeastern University.

As an administrator at one of the leading school systems in Georgia, she became a voice for children who were being left behind in the mainstream academic setting. She retired from the school system to fulfill a lifetime goal of establishing The Benjamin Preschool of Academic and Performing Arts in Smyrna, Georgia. Her passion to support children facing challenges led her to author a book, *Health Intelligence,* a work that grapples with the core issues causing obesity crisis among children. Her interest in children's health inspired her to develop the Healthy Benji series of children's books focused on establishing healthy eating habits in children.

Dr. Benjamin-Lambert is the mother of four successful girls and the grandmother to four boys. She enjoys life with her best friend and loving husband, Harry Lambert, Jr., in Kennesaw, Georgia. She is proud to be a citizen of the United States but returns to Jamaica quite frequently to visit her mother and father, Pearly Mae and Albert Benjamin, who she thanks for serving as strong role models for her and her eight siblings.